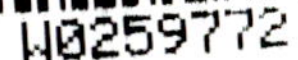

TOUCH TO AFFLICTION

NATHALIE STEPHENS

COACH HOUSE BOOKS | TORONTO

first edition

Canada Council for the Arts | Conseil des Arts du Canada

Published with the assistance of the Canada Council for the Arts and the Ontario Arts Council. We also acknowledge the financial support of the Government of Canada through the Book Publishing Industry Development Program.

LIBRARY AND ARCHIVES CANADA CATALOGUING IN PUBLICATION

Stephens, Nathalie, 1970-
Touch to affliction / Nathalie Stephens.

Poems.
ISBN-13: 978-1-55245-175-5
ISBN-10: 1-55245-175-5

1. Excavations (Archaeology)--Poetry. I. Title.

PS8587.T375T69 2006 C811'.54 C2006-903523-7

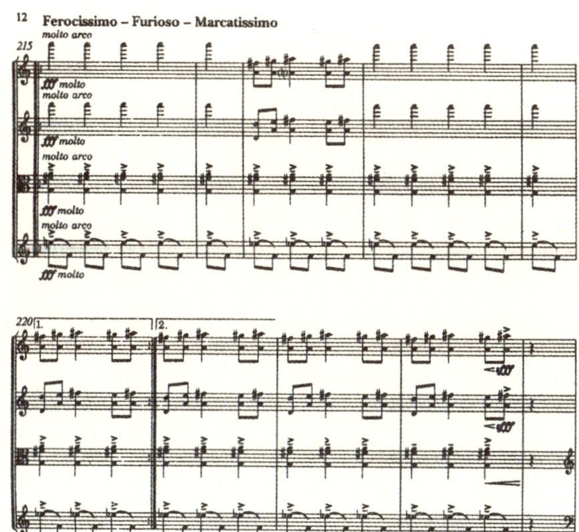

'Już się̨zmierzcha' ('Already It Is Dusk')
from *String Quartet No. 1, Opus 62*
– Henryk Mikołaj Górecki

TOUCH TO AFFLICTION

We are walking backward into our lives. Our cities are incensed. They fester on our thighs. And we lick at them in garish immoderate delight.

When colour comes we run. We have no idea why.

§

There are bodies inside bodies inside bodies.

Not just you. The small body with you. The tooth-scraped sand-blasted body.

See how big it has become.

§

Le Poème Affligé

Let me tell you some of what I have seen. Amid the languages I speak and those I keep concealed. Things I have touched with my hands and those that have eluded me.

Through a window in an old wooden door the sky breaks at dusk. What remains is a dark stain where none was. And my inability to recall the shape of things before.

There is a telephone with a cut cord and a dog lying heavily against the wall. It is or is not cold.

I walk from one end of a room to another.

I walk from one end of a garden to another.

What remains after seeing is a short burst of colour, gone.

After suggests something other. Other than what is before me. This letter, your name.

Language that is conciliatory rebukes the body. I am offended by the nature of words and their ability to dissuade. Often I am most offended by the words of your language. The language in which I write. The language that sets my body against itself. And dismantles the present.

In your language, there is illusion, but there is no hope.

In hope, there is illusion.

And in illusion, there is the stuff of language.

I have acquired a viola that in time I will learn to play. Do you still listen to Górecki? I have also acquired the score to 'Already It Is Dusk.' In it, Górecki notes: 'The viola is always "en dehors," but not too much.' Do you know what this means? I believe it to mean that the viola for Górecki is much as some poets intend language to be. The viola is always underneath the music. Underneath is the suggestion of itself. It is outside. In another language I would say: Désincarné. But I would not say: Disembodied.

Affliction is a capital word. Affliction is the blood of poetry.

Don't misunderstand me. Through the window in the door, I see the afflicted sky. It is afflicted because it is out of reach. For a poet, this too might be the nature of language. And it might also be the nature of the poet, in relation to others. For the poet must make language into two things simultaneously: sobriety and passion. Does not Buber do the same through Walter Kaufmann?

'And to gain freedom from the belief in unfreedom is to gain freedom.'

Where is the poet who will return language to the body?

Where is the body that is prepared to receive language?

I am sending you plays by Koltès. I think that you will know what I mean.

My Thigh Grew a City

I went into a new city with old words.

A river swallowed a lake. An iron bridge swerved and hooked the sky. The names of streets scattered.

Three held passion.

I bit into a wooden rail. Water rose to where I stood. A strangulated swamp and gold and granite. Books.

I carried a small body in my teeth.

Claim nothing as your own. Not curvature. Nor comfort. Nor sleep.

I wanted fracture. I wanted fleeting. I wanted feign. The city bore into bone. The wound opened onto sound. The sound echoed and echoed into the small body and cringing hands and settled on a stone step and I said nothing. 'Nothing.' Wept.

Inside memory is little worth keeping. Matchsticks. Some loose change. And the frayed edges of your city. Frayed because of memory. I am trying not to touch it too often, nor imagine it too fiercely.

Inside memory is the failure of memory. I go there and come upon my arrogance at wanting the thing that language won't offer. What your language says as distinctly as mine. What is wanting. What is reach. Language does not beckon. It scoffs. Inside your city with its vengeful rivers and wrought bridges. When it says 'I love,' it knocks holes into the riverbed.

We will drown in the city and we will take our languages with us.

Desire is not a measure for speaking. One man leans into another man and this man catches the first in a quiet embrace. The street sounds dissipate. The smokestacks cough rings into the city. The rail lines buckle and break.

I am that man and I am both leaning and not leaning.

The city is this city.

The train is late.

I wait for the tall light to amber. I listen to the feather weight of fall. I reach into the bone collapse of grief. And the stranger reach for me.

My eyes move from the man's mouth to the orange sky.

The city catches fire.

And we are in it.

§

The body is small and familiar.
It is a small body and it is familiar (to me).

I sit near the body with my hands placed on the small chest and the small back. I warm the cold legs. I stroke the small head. The eyes are wide with fear. The eyes are wide with fear.

With fear.

In your language, to attach a word to a thing is to resist the thing.

Instead I touch it with my hands until my hands are thick with touching and the colour is gone from the eyes and the head twitches and my hands are noise and trembling until the wind pushes the door and the wood marks bruises on my wrists and my wrists snap and the fingers come to rest against the insides of my arms and my knees burrow into concrete and the small body becomes heavy and the lungs expel liquid and the heaving moves from the body into the room and the window on the door shatters and the heart hooks into the ribs and the blood drains from the face and the clay runs down the wall and the house hunches against the earth and the jaw cracks and the animals are silent and the air twitches and a dog refuses food and a machine whirs and a river overflows and the thing catches me not sleeping.

§

Do you notice that it is dusk every time we look into the city?

That two hands pressed eagerly against a glass pane are a form of scripture. That the impression left by a city is carved from bone. That the language of a city is a language that mourns. And inside mourning are two lips mouthing no words and they swallow the city whole. You call this faith. I call this savagery. And we are getting nowhere with and without our languages. Our bodies breaking form.

My body is the place where the city began.

The city with its grief and its hammered stone.

Ces ruines I would say but it isn't my turn to speak.

Ces ruines I would say but I would be speaking for someone else.

I imagine words other than those from which I was grown.

I don't tell you reasons for grieving nor a posture for scorn. What I see is indiscernible. And I hesitate to move at all. The soft burn of metal pushing through flesh. A ridge of streaking scars. One line indicating another or the tug of skin on some sharp thing. Is this memory? This is what springs from earth. It is another kind of geography. It is memory pulling away from memory. It is the violence of a city. It is the misdeed of language. Or the unspeaking body.

I wrote you a book of meaning. It contained the vestiges of a language.

In time, you said.

The Jews of Attali held it in their own hands and measured its validity, worth. The pages of the book wore through. A skin shrinking from bone. Not a hooking into. Rather a sinking through. We were white with dust and our lips moved in red.

Language coloured us and the book bled. So what does this say about meaning and the skin rubbed from our fingers?

These are questions for you and they are not.

A painted line runs over the earth. And we stand aside until it makes its way to us. Then we run.

As we run our hands turn to blood and our mouths dry. The book catches fire and this is as we read it.

We leave a place for fear and we bear it.

If, for example.

The desert changes shape.

Do not think that the prairie doesn't.

I was to be a hermaphrodite. Caught in my own sex or in between. My thigh grew a city. My hands held a river. Someone walked through me. We all drowned.

If I were a Jew, would you love me more or less?

In time, you said.

If, for example.

The question is always wrong. The book is always misplaced. Give me a dissonant body. I will understand that the earth is misshapen and my own name forgotten.

In any country, there is a field and it is surrounded by wire that is barbed. La barbarie is infectious. On your tongue it is beautiful, and you are already dead.

This is what my language said in reply.

This is what my book concealed.

And so I burned it.

And so we bled.

And a flame hides nothing of what burns.

And my thigh still grows a city.

And you will not name it.

§

It is not possible in your language to grieve. To touch the lungs that collapse or the bones that break. Water pouring from an unbreathing mouth. It is not a matter of words for things. Rather it is a matter of distance between the word and the thing.

§

Not Paris

I want to know: What part of you remains inconsolable?

If these are letters to myself, the names beside them are thin screens of hope. Perhaps. The tear is visible.

What part of fear is not attached to a name? What part of a name does not beckon exile? What part of exile does not disavow living?

A city's worth is a consequence of its bookshops and architecture. And its capacity to withstand suffering.

Our cities are well worn and there is beauty showing through. Their languages are sooty and they are delirious with crumbling.

On the name of each city is a layer of dust. Underneath the dust is nothing much.

Is the dust what we came for?

For begins the words forgotten and forlorn. It is possible to mount a history of a place on the inconsistent edges of letters. Our history, if there is such a thing as a shared history, might slide into the crook of an 'r' and remain wedged there for a time.

There is little to say in answer to that.

Nonetheless I will say this: I am entering into an old alphabet with no words. I may emerge with fewer still.

These months I have walked through three cities. Each city had its rivers for drowning, and lovers stood at their edges. First came the jolt of recognition. Then the shame that comes with knowing.

Out loud I spoke words of one language and then of another.

Two hands covered my mouth and a body rose from water. I reached for it and fell.

On my knees the earth was quiet and the wind blew over me.

This is what your language will not give me.

The thing that is breaking. The thing that is known.

Simone Weil was dead before she was dying. When she was still Jacob.

Words came away from her tongue and her pen was insolent with knowing. She was mad.

Her body tore from its canvas. She found nothing in the thing she desired.

Le vide is not nothing.

Weil's language was a language of not meaning.

She left room for the thing that was breaking.

She slept with her head against a pile of stones.

In Paris, the Seine overflows and corpses wash onto its shores. The tourists board the bateaux-mouches. The sky fills with buzzards. And the Levites gnash their teeth.

Le corps is not the same as corpse. And this is not Paris. But it's close enough.

Your language gives me order. It says nothing of la douleur.

I take it into my hands as I would a large stone and I drop it into water.

What wants seeing and the small body with it rises from under.

Finitude Lamentation

Who cries out anymore?

This arms askew dwindling and furor.

This inconsequential.

This river torn weary and walking behind.

This fantasy touching the curve of gentle.

This finitude lamentation.

This gridded this untraced stoppable.

You bent a body into language. It ran arrested ran.

Accented is a disturbance. It is a kind of convulsion. Language anguishing over the mouth that it might hold.

I am no landscape. I am the visage of a sacrilege. I carry shattered idols in my throat. And ungodlike.

Plunder what is known.

There is inside (of me) a distinction. Is a collision. Is an apology. Commas in between.

Stop me.

Inside your language there is a word that means sleep. In my mouth it is a broken jaw gaping. Is a wide sigh heaving. Is plated armour. Hammer blow. Bone. La langue is un fléau.

Abandon. Stuttering. Torn.

Is a distinction:

A grotto, cleft.

Is a collision:

I do not say my language any more than I say my body.
I do not long for either.

I rue the many avenues of suffering but can name none.

Is an apology:

Is not meaning.

Shames me into knowing. This unsleeping noiseless mouthing. This fanaticism desperate unbelieving.

This two fingers sewn together tearing.

Agonize.

Is equal parts of Arvo Pärt and Walter Benjamin.

Crystalline and severing.

You identify me as a contested surface. A stripped margin of land. A divergence of affinities. A pillage.

The vestiges therefore. A destructive force. When I speak I am broken-jaw stutter. A stain on the surface of longing.

I say: I do not long for either.

What I mean is: From whose language must I speak?

Not confessional. Evidence, rather, of the unspeakable. That thing toward which we move and we are an affront to the language we use to name it.

Sleep is not a kind of death. It is a paralysis. An overturned cavity. It is bloodless. That does not make it free.

In your language the present erases itself. You stand in a place and the present comes and you are not standing there anymore. The book in your hand is a grimace on the face of some reader. And your hand is a stone in water. These are pictures, maybe. Inaccuracies. What you remember is a small square of paper organized into pixels. Your language does not remember. And when you say 'What was,' you are already falling away.

L'oubli is the word you are searching for. The word outside of which you disappear. I am again with your language and le vide. Le vide is not nothing. Your language is not traceable. So what does your present hold?

This is as I might speak. But want is otherwise configured. And there is the question of memory. The timing is all wrong.

Your language might be a stilled beat. An inopportune rhyme. Afflicting these bodies. I say these because we are several at least and we will populate our deaths as we populate our cities: Feverishly.

§

The body is a small discrepancy.

The small body is smaller still.

And the hands that weigh grief are implacable.

The mouth, though, is in agony. Pulling sound from sound.

The picture is of a city drowning. This is you, over here, and me, I am just off to the side and I am laughing.

Laughing says head thrown back or it does not.

Night falls with a crash on the dead and we walk crunching snow and the dogs chew bones.

We place the small body into the river. The river is ice and our eyes grow cold. The wind cuts into our skin. We run fingers over ridges of bone. We do not recognize what is torn. We go back to the city. We demand reparations. We hold our knuckles to the light. The snow thickens. The sky catches what we throw. We bury ourselves in rubble. In time night turns over into some other thing. The river breaks against us. We fall and we fall. We are foolish and we break inside language. The city groans. We are not lovers. There is nowhere to go. The dogs carry us in their teeth. They take us there and it is so cold.

§

Broyer as with Centuries or Meat

The thing came at me in this precise way: as the face. The face on a small body perhaps. As the small body falls from the arms. This is the face of Lévinas and as such your language without a philosophy of hunger is incomplete. Without a philosophy of touch. Without a philosophy of greed. And so on.

The face of Lévinas appears as two eyes commanding murder and fragility.

Touch what wants touching and you will break alongside the thing you would hold if in your language there were moments for breath and the capacity to yearn.

Lévinas is not your language.

And you have yet to speak.

Leaving. Not so much as having.

You wish yourself out of arms' reach the way you wish yourself out of your city. There is logic in bereavement but decry worship. The way your city was thrust from your thigh and what was wine ran like night through bone that is implacable. The night sky is cock-hard moving over you. And water on your tongue is nothing like fire, but dirt.

This theology bears the weight of every untraceable sadness.

What your language touches moves. What moves beckons murder. And what is murdered scratches a worn whisper onto all the faces.

Geography is conversion. A measure for what is lost.

We were looking up at ourselves.

With our texts full of faces and our hands like water getting into everything.

Do you know the word broyer?

As with stone or chicken gut.

In it is the turbine with its axle and teeth. Death count. Or le cri.

Broyer as with centuries or meat.

Broyer as with morality.

A garden beneath a darkening sky.

A dog heavily.

Lévinas cries out, why wouldn't he?

Geography is perversion.

Lyon, 1987: Klaus Barbie's name is on la place publique and in so many mouths. Like this against a French tonsil and chattering teeth. Summer is the dismantled scaffolding of the Palais de Justice. This is as time reconstitutes itself. For Klaus Barbie it is always summer. Even with the heat he does not weep. He smiles for the camera. And the little girl who is eighty-one.

All this time his hair grew and saliva wet his tongue.

What is relevant is not memory but its absence. Is not habit but its betrayal. Is not innovation but humility. Is not love but anguish. Is not literature but history. Is not language but sediment. Is not amnesty.

Is grievous.

Is grievous.

Is grievous.

Communion is cannibalism.

Steiner's century is closed to further inspection and our books are little else than capsules of complacency.

An upheld hand is a shield for the face an admonishment a plea at times and often threatening. Une menace.

The hand of Amichai is shattered bone and Darwish with him laps water from cups of stone.

We Are Accountable for What We Aren't Told

Your language like your country. I speak poorly.

I haven't deference for the past. Nor its beginnings. Our languages behave as poorly as we do. This talk of peace. The mouth's ecology. Devastation.

And I want to know: Who are we defending?

What do we learn?

Of futility. Of machines. Of discouragement. Of condemnation.

A country is four corners of earth draped over bone and as much silence as water can hold. Initiations to war.

Homeland is patrie and the sands are incensed by the crush of feet and the city groans from centuries of stone and our voices erode what sense to l'oubli. Forget it, I say. Oublie. What everything we know. I am reading Said and the bones break in my feet. Like this walking into the century and dry earth underneath.

Let me explain.

I am ignorant of my enemies and my face has many origins.

What part of you is city?

The mouth straying from speech. The hand from other hands. The hip from sleep. L'ahurissement.

The body you imagined keeping. The sentence, fourfold.

What part of you is famine?

The distance from the body is a sacrilege. It is a cleaner word for fall. It speaks the suddenness of dust. And what wings tear. And what skin splits. And what claims the viscera. I am in it with mes doigts. The small body on the windowsill. And the waiting sounds below.

We are prohibition. Our skin strips. Our bloodless. And we are aghast at what we keep. What citystruck we keep. The wrought-iron bridges. The candied animals. The drone.

Night is vertiginous.

City is fosse commune.

'Et vous, vous ne m'embrassez pas?'

Juan Bourla is a voice recorded on paper. A room filled with smoke. History is provocation. His mouth is greedy for sleep. To Lise he is a body in shadow. To Simone de Beauvoir he is what remains unseen.

In Bourla's Paris, it is always 1943. The rail lines anticipate stone.

This is as our languages recoil. This is what the mouth abhors. The fastening of suffering to the lettermost forlorn. Is this as madness is meant to be? The simple dislocation of city from bone. As though what was impassioned could not be borne. As though what was chaste were close enough to living.

I want a mind sensorial. A figure awoken from sleep. The haze in waking is perhaps troublesome, deep. It certainly is burdensome, and our mouths become slow. But if the city were wordless, if the pavement broke, what manner for walking, what need for breach?

‘These bodies.’

Those were not your exact words. I took them into me.

The ocean is a measure for grief. What drowned letters and memory, relief.

Reli*ef*. How France became l’Algérie and the winter that brought snow carried the shame of leaving (being made to leave) and the detritus of speech. The remaining words stuck to the tongue. The thing burns in and outside of us. And our blooded knees are the only possible trajectory. This reaching along and touching through. As though our bodies were simpler even than desire or the ability to speak.

Speak. It begins in the throat of a boy and the refusal to ancestry. It begins in the names on the registry and the subsequent ratages. And these ashes on my desk and the voices that end. What has language to offer that the earth cannot hold?

These are simple diversions. Great claims of hope or no hope at all. And our mouths move around sounds shovelled into the ground below.

Our century (this one, the one before) appeases itself with confession.

We are ungainly and stubborn.

We have read too many books.

We mistake ourselves for those we abandon.

We deign to fall.

What permissions have been granted?

What languages received?

Kristof and her truncated country on a mouth in short sentences. Dib and his displaced ancestry, the culled strangers on unnamed streets. (France, always France.)

Am I that progeny?

What brings the body tremble or weep?

What language with its difficulties enables me to speak?

We are new to suffering. What we claim as home is fantasme. We are weak. We speak clumps of hair and loose teeth. We peer at things from below with our arms to steady our fall.

Is this what we call English? The permission to retreat?

Your language deliberately.

August 1988: The Golfe de Gascogne collapses red tile two hands and a small room atop a flight of stairs. The mountains: proximity. The beach: sleet. Un baiser: reproachful. What dreamt what meant keep. A measure too full of landscape. Fistfully. You imagine sunswept fellatio feux d'artifice. Il n'en est rien.

Rien. What drowns in winter survives sleep. What wrists on a quai de gare bleed. What holds sound in a small tile again and over. Fisted. A city. Impossible to keep. J'ai. Je n'ai.

This is as I dreamt language. This is dream is séquelles is fine is fine is ask me anything from now on. Not chronology.

And what you will believe.

Simply: The city turns grey and disappears. The body wants dédommagement for the things it sees. It goes on seeing. Your language accounts for none of it. We are young. We are only witnesses if we are willing to speak. But what language will hold us? What temperament for fugitif?

L'abattoir or la place publique. Slaughter is someone's reverie. And we are wallowing in meat.

Place is manquement is not missing.

What we touch is aberration but we go on touching and what we turn over reddens in the sun and weakens in the rain and everything is bone and everything is dust and brick is water that is weatherworn so that we drown in masonry and trowel is layering and we bury ourselves willingly and we touch the facades of so many buildings with our fingers catching nails and our skin unbleeding the door posts the iron scaffoldings the misery and what trembles (ce qui tremble) is not pretty and nostalgia is idiocy is yearning is mediocrity is not pathos or figurative is this wall is how many missing and what have we done?

Plainly: I have counted my dead and they far outnumber me.

§

Language's impudence, certainly. Wear words the way you wear your city.

Brash. Inconvenienced. Alight.

A bruise is city-lust. A record of having been. You are bent over a ledger, pen-press of ink, indelible.

Water runs into you.

I am your city. I am that impulsive. That wounded. That bludgeoned. Grief-struck, perhaps. And in this exchange, this tracing, this losing ourselves and we never turn up, are the banished realms of happiness, the truth-sought furrows into earth, and the capping, again and again, of trust.

The small body shudders with the earth. We are witnesses and that is all. We dare to measure ourselves against our cities. And we are right. We are that forceful, that wanton, that murderous. When we weep, we are inconsolable. Our grief is that barbaric.

§

The Scarceness of the Body Architecture's Scorn

Here is where we begin. It is a distortion of ici and always fleeting. What we touch upon is the better part of leaving. We are dizzy with wanting and the paper-thin wrapper of sleep, le vertige.

The cities will drive out their poets. With our battered fists and our broken feet we will trample their streets.

Nous traversions la même ville.

River is wheat. We pull water from earth and wet our teeth. What breaks is already broken. What speaks cannot speak.

Hand is fracture is remnant is see.

What could Wagner have possibly known about Sprache about Juif?

Is this what our languages tell us?

What is scriptural is proscription is bleak.

Earth is rapture. Maybe. Un silence pour tout recouvrir. And skin is the finest trajectory. But what tears tears again is not a matter of mending but soupir.

Ici is where we might have been is deep sky rent by mandibles is hue is magnitude is screen.

Geography is coercion.

What we touch we touch unwittingly.

What body is wanting is fuite. Your language in my city and every indecency. We are fragile and this is as we speak.

Forgive me. Your language, it is in me. We were saying, interrupted, and the city, with its echo, unanswering.

Is not translatability. So I won't say: Translate me. Nor: Read me instead. Is the thing that might or might not be dead. Is a stone arch, a metal rail, an overgrown waterway.

It is always possible to drown in the mouth that doesn't close, in the faint sound that follows after breath, in the thing that falls away from itself. If we turn away, our books will burn and our cities will drown, much in the way blood runs from the body.

Do you know the word sombrer? It is dark and watery and deep inside what things we keep.

This is as your language swallows me. Inside its creviced simplicity. Not so much what's missing as what lies underneath.

I am in between leaving. With and against your language inevitably.

The thing distances itself

in the rusted rail line

in the river's avarice

in the heron's seamless reach.

Inside the city is the insufficiency of grieving, the singularity of bone, some interrupted movement. Le jaillissement and whatever holds us down.

I said city.

I didn't say keep.

I prodded what wanted prodding. With my boneless fingers, with my temperamental voice, with my illegitimacy.

The body that wanted burying shattered against me. The reach that wanted collapsing disappeared from view. And the wistfulness in the dry branches of fallen trees dissuaded me from leaning into the thing that might appease.

City is stone, yes, but it is stone that is worn. It is skin that falls away from bone. It is the thing we go toward. It is the thing and that is all. We haven't a name for it. It is that maddening. It is that forlorn.

What is city is remains and the slow river widens and the ruelles become constricted and the bodies in their skins with their broad hands touch water that is sullied and drink it into them.

These are your dead.

They are the stone walls, the misshapen walkways, the insurmountable inclines, the moss-grown crevices, the stained brick, and the métro with its thin scream pulling over metal, its rattle of boxes from station to station, its injurious rail. What is city is vociferous and batters the body, your body and mine. It is the city in its body and it is very much alive. It pulls what it pushes. It lives against you. And it walks with you in your hobbled legs and your collapsing reach. City is here and it is the place where you have yet to go.

As for your language it is what empties from your mouth and that is all. It is what I mean by mutisme and folie at times. There is a word for incomplete and it begins inside.

NOS LANGUES SONT INCOMMENSURABLES ET MEURTRIÈRES

(OUR LANGUAGES ARE INFINITE AND MURDEROUS)

Ne demandez pas après moi. Cette faim. Une infâme solitude. L'arrimage de l'être au passage des êtres enclins à la disparition. À l'horreur que nous sommes vous et moi. Un corps géographiquement situé au bord de sa peau aux bords rabattus d'un hameau, à la torpeur d'une baise insignifiante, ces boutures de désir colmatées en une peau barbare. On a deux mains pour ramasser ce qu'on laisse tomber, pour tout jeter à l'eau. Figure-toi que j'ai honte pour nous et je touche à ce qui ne bouge. Comme c'est crasseux le lieux où tu vas. | Fistfully. Mouthfully. The place you take into you is an injury and my prints are all over you. This is your city. Your tawdry. As though speaking of seeing could correct calamity. Our limbs are not limber. And geography cringes at the encroachment of further geography. Find the text that granted permission, the book that wanted burning, the mouth that needed closing, the hand held before an expressionless face. Brazen and stumbling.

Notes and Acknowledgements

Parts of *Touch To Affliction* have been published in variously altered forms in *Shift & Switch: New Canadian Poetry* (The Mercury Press, 2005), *Pissing Ice: An Anthology of 'New' Canadian Poets* (BookThug, 2004), *A Common Sky: Canadian Writers Against the War* (Three Square Press, 2003), *New American Writing* (2005), *Action Yes Online Quarterly*, *dANDelion*, *Senez*, *filling Station*, *jubilat* and *Tessera*, and by Nº Press and above/ground press.

The author acknowledges the assistance of the Ontario Arts Council.

About the Author

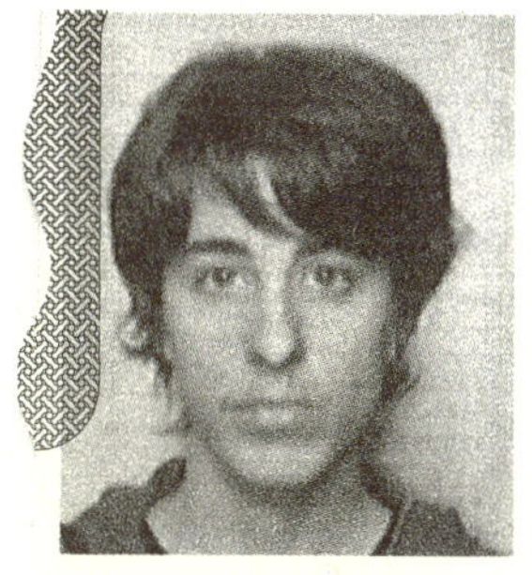

Nathalie Stephens writes l'entre-genre in English and French. She is the author of a dozen books including *Paper City* (2003), *Je Nathanaël* (2003) and *L'Injure* (2004), a finalist of the Prix Alain-Grandbois and the Prix Trillium. *Je Nathanaël* exists in English self-translation with BookThug (2006). Other work exists in Basque and Slovene with book-length translations forthcoming in Bulgarian. Imminent with Nota Bene is an essay of correspondence entitled *L'absence au lieu: Claude Cahun et le livre inouvert.*

Stephens is (in) a city of bridges.

Works by Nathalie Stephens

You But For The Body Fell Against (Belladonna, 2005)
The Small Body With It Rises From Under (No Press, 2005)
L'Injure (l'Hexagone, 2004)
Held (abrégé) (above/ground press, 2004)
Paper City (Coach House Books, 2003)
Je Nathanaël (l'Hexagone, 2003; BookThug, 2006)
Grammaire des sens (housepress, 2002)
What Exile This (above/ground press, 2002)
L'embrasure (Éditions TROIS, 2002)
There Is No Object Between Us (housepress, 2001)
All Boy (housepress, 2001; BookThug, 2004)
Somewhere Running (Arsenal Pulp Press, 2000)
Underground (Éditions TROIS, 1999)
Colette m'entends-tu? (Éditions TROIS, 1997)
This Imagined Permanence (Gutter Press, 1996)
hivernale (Éditions du GREF, 1995)

Typeset in Charlotte and Charlotte Sans
Printed and bound at the Coach House on bpNichol Lane, 2006.

Edited for the press by Stephen Motika
Designed by Alana Wilcox
Cover design by Rick/Simon
Cover image by Jeff Marlin (detail from *Untitled Painting*, acrylic on canvas, 10" x 10", 2006), courtesy of the artist

Coach House Books
401 Huron Street on bpNichol Lane
Toronto, Ontario M5S 2G5
Canada

416 979 2217
800 367 6360

mail@chbooks.com
www.chbooks.com